ANDROMACHE

ANDROMACHE

GILBERT MURRAY

ISBN: 978-93-5420-117-2

Published: 1900

ANDROMACHE
A PLAY IN THREE ACTS

BY

GILBERT MURRAY

MDCCCC

CONTENTS

PREFATORY LETTER.

My Dear ARCHER,

The germ of this play sprang into existence on a certain April day in 1896 which you and I spent chiefly in dragging our reluctant bicycles up the great hills that surround Riveaulx Abbey, and discussing, so far as the blinding rain allowed us, the questions whether all sincere comedies are of necessity cynical, and how often we had had tea since the morning, and how far it would be possible to treat a historical subject loyally and unconventionally on a modern stage. Then we struck (as, I fear, is too often the fate of those who converse with me) on the subject of the lost plays of the Greek tragedians. We talked of the extraordinary variety of plot that the Greek dramatist found in his historical tradition, the force, the fire, the depth and richness of character-play. We thought of the marvellous dramatic possibilities of an age in which actual and living heroes and sages were to be seen moving against a background of primitive superstition and blank savagery; in which the soul of man walked more free from trappings than seems ever to have been permitted to it since. But I must stop; I see that I am approaching the common pitfall of playwrights who venture upon prefaces, and am beginning to prove how good my play ought to be!

What I want to remind you of is this: that we agreed that a simple historical play, with as little convention as possible, placed in the Greek Heroic Age, and dealing with one of the ordinary heroic stories, ought to be, well, an interesting experiment. Beyond this point, I know, we began to differ. You wanted verse and the Greece of the English poets. I wanted, above all things, a nearer approach to my conception of the real Greece, the Greece of history and even—dare I say it?—of anthropology! I recognise your full right to disapprove of every word and every sentiment of this play from the first to the last, but I hope you will not grudge me the pleasure of associating your name with at least the inception of the experiment, and thanking you at the same time for the many gifts of friendly encouragement and stimulating objurgation which you have bestowed upon

Yours sincerely,
GILBERT MURRAY.

January 1900.

DRAMATIS PERSONÆ

PYRRHUS	*Son of Achilles; King of Phthia.*
ANDROMACHE	*Once wife of Hector, Prince of Troy; now slave to Pyrrhus.*
HERMIONE	*Daughter of Helen, Queen of Sparta; wife to Pyrrhus.*
MOLOSSUS	*Child of Pyrrhus and Andromache.*
ALCIMEDON *or* ALCIMUS	*An old Captain of Achilles' Myrmidons.*
ORESTES	*Son of Agamemnon, King of Mycenæ; now banished for the slaying of his mother, Clytæmnestra.*
PYLADES	*A Prince of Phocis, friend to Orestes.*
A PRIEST OF THETIS	
TWO MAIDS OF HERMIONE	

Certain Maidens, Myrmidons, Men-at-Arms.

The Action takes place in Phthia, on the Southern borders of Thessaly, about fifteen years after the Fall of Troy.

ANDROMACHE

THE FIRST ACT

SCENE: *The coast of Phthia. Rocks at the back, with the sea visible behind them. One of the rocks is a shrine, having niches cut in it for receiving offerings. On the right in front is the Altar of Thetis, shrouded in trees; to the left, a well. A path to the left leads to* PYRRHUS' *castle; another, far back to the right, leads to the house of the* PRIEST. *It is the morning twilight, with a faint glimmer of dawn.*

At the foot of the rock ORESTES *is seated in meditation; he carries two spears, and wears the garb of a traveller. An* ARMED MAN *is moving off the stage at the back, as though going towards the sea; he stops suddenly, listens, and hides behind a rock.*

Enter, coming up from the sea, PYLADES, *armed.*
The MAN *steps out.*

MAN.

My lord Pylades.

PYLADES.

Where have you left him?

MAN.

Yonder, by the shrine. He bade me go back to the ship.

PYLADES.

[*Crossing to* ORESTES.] Is it too late to turn your purpose?

ORESTES.

[*As though half roused from his reverie.*] I seek only to see if she is indeed so passing beautiful. She was; I am sure she was, until—— [*He pauses.*

PYLADES.

Let me go first and spy out a way for you.

ORESTES.

[*With sudden resentment.*] You think I am still mad!

PYLADES.

Nay, no more mad than I, but more quick to anger. It would be safer for me to go.

ORESTES.

You think I am still mad because I dared not say it! I will say it here by the altar. [*Doggedly.*] I will see if she is still as she used to be before the day when—[*with effort*]—I shed my mother's blood, and first saw——

PYLADES.

Speak not Their name, brother. You did nought but the gods' plain bidding. You see them no more now that you are healed.

ORESTES.

'Twas you that feared to name them, not I!

PYLADES.

Nay, you fear nothing; that is why I must fear for you.

ORESTES.

What is there to fear for me? Most like I shall come back just as I am.

PYLADES.

That is the one thing that cannot be!

ORESTES.

[*Musingly.*] If she is changed as all the world else is changed since that time—— [*Abruptly.*] I care not for the woman. I will come back. If not—— [*Smiles ambiguously.*

PYLADES.

But why go alone, and why venture so much? We two could lie hid in the thickets by the shrine yonder, and see her when the women come to pray at sunrise. And then——

ORESTES.

[*With determination, interrupting him.*] I will go alone, and see her and speak with her alone! Hinder me not, friend! Leave no man to watch over me. Keep the ship well hidden, and have twoscore men ambushed above the cliff, to hold the path if need comes.

PYLADES.

There shall be fourscore ever ready to your call, night or day.

MAN.

[*Coming down from path at back.*] My chief, the dawn is drawing close.

ORESTES.

Ay, get you gone before any worshippers come.

PYLADES.

As you will, then. And Apollo be your guard!

> [*Exeunt* PYLADES *and* ARMED MAN. ORESTES *wraps his mantle round him and sits in silence.*]

> *Enter from the right,* PRIEST *of Thetis, with a bowl in his hands. He climbs a rock at the back and watches the sunrise.*

PRIEST.

Not yet. Not quite yet. Ah, there it catches the crag-top: now the trees:—yes, there is the glint far off upon the sea! [*Comes down towards the shrine and prays.*] Hail, Thetis! Accept this wine and honey I bring thee at first touch of dawn. Keep thy Priest in wealth and honour, even as I keep thy worship. And, as the sunlight drives the Things of darkness from thy waters—— [*Seeing* ORESTES.] Averter of evil! Who is this that has sat through the darkness under the Holy Rock? Stranger, whence come you here?

ORESTES.

From Acarnania. Have I sinned in resting here?

PRIEST.

No man of Phthia, for his life, would stay here in darkness! Saw you not anything?

ORESTES.

What should I see?

PRIEST.

No changing manifold shapes, as of women or winged things?

ORESTES.

[*Harshly.*] I saw nought but what I have seen on a thousand nights. Enough! If I have offended any goddess I will make amends.

> [*He begins to wring off a pendant from a gold chain that he wears,*

and moves towards the altar.

PRIEST.

Stay! There is no blood upon your hands?

ORESTES.

I have slain a man.

PRIEST.

How long since? Is the stain washed off?

ORESTES.

Oh, I have been purified and purified!

PRIEST.

Duly and fully—with hyssop and the blood of swine?

ORESTES.

With better sacrifices than swine! I am clean enough to make amends to your goddess. [*Coming across to the shrine.*] Where shall I lay it? For I may need her favour. [*Holds out the gold pendant.*

PRIEST.

[*Surprised.*] Gold! Stranger, it is well to give gold to Thetis, but——

ORESTES.

Well, I give it to Thetis!

PRIEST.

Scarce a man in Phthia has ever touched gold, save Pyrrhus himself and the servants of Hermione. Nor many, I should guess, in Acarnania.

ORESTES.

A banished man must have his wealth in little compass.

PRIEST.

A chain like that should buy an exile's return.

ORESTES.

I care not to return.

PRIEST.

Are the friends of the dead so bitter against you?

ORESTES.

The friends of the dead are dead, and my friends are dead. I have none to fear; but I have been wronged, my house taken from me, and my father's wealth, and the woman that was vowed me to wife. No more, old man! I am an exile, and I live in happier lands than mine own.

PRIEST.

Is it in Phthia you seek for a happy land? No matter; affliction comes to the good as to the evil.

ORESTES.

Why, what ails your city, if a stranger may know?

PRIEST.

See you that shrine, and the footprint of Thetis in the rock? Once it was all covered with offerings!

ORESTES.

It is not so well loaded, nor yet so ill. Is there no worse than that?

PRIEST.

Worse? Barren fields and a barren queen, and hatred in the house of Achilles!

ORESTES.

Is it some sin the King has done?

PRIEST.

The King and a woman.

ORESTES.

[*Starting.*] Has *that* sin met its punishment? Speak plainly, Priest.

PRIEST.

Long years ago, Pyrrhus brought back from Troy a slave woman to share his bed.

ORESTES.

[*As though reassured.*] Hector's wife, Andromache, men say.

PRIEST.

The wife of his father's bitterest enemy! Ay, and she was his enemy too, and loathed her life with Pyrrhus.

ORESTES.

They all struggle, these women captives. But what harm came of it?

PRIEST.

She is a foe to the land and to Thetis!

ORESTES.

But has he not cast her off? [*With constraint.*] Men say he has wedded a new Queen, the daughter of Helen.

PRIEST.

Oh, the Trojan has not dwelt in the King's house these ten years back. She begged him for a hut in the mountain, and he gave it her.

ORESTES.

She begged to be sent away! How was that?

PRIEST.

Why should a woman wish to live in secret, and not be seen? [*Slight pause.*] There be wise women among the barbarians.

ORESTES.

Wise in bad drugs and magic; I know no other wisdom in them.

PRIEST.

You have said it! There is a prophet here who knows of counter-charms—I gave him three ewes for this that I wear—[*showing a charm made of wolves' teeth*]— else I durst not face her!

ORESTES.

Whom has she chiefly hurt?

PRIEST.

Men say she has waked the dead Hector to come to her across the seas! [*He shudders.*] But for the King, we should have judged her long ago.

ORESTES.

Does the new Queen hate her?

PRIEST.

Has she not blighted the womb of the Queen? There is no heir to Achilles in Achilles' land!

ORESTES.

And does Pyrrhus sit still while his Queen is thus wronged?

PRIEST.

Cannot a witch blind the eyes? He can see nothing, and will hearken to nothing. Even now he has taken the Trojan woman's bastard with him.

ORESTES.

Is Pyrrhus away from the land? Where?

PRIEST.

He has gone hunting in the hills yonder—[*pointing*]—and down to the fields of the Napæans.

ORESTES.

When should he return?

PRIEST.

To-day, it may be—it is the fifth day of the hunt; or perchance the game may keep him some time yet. [*Enter* ALCIMEDON, L., *an old man with spears but no armour; he carries a bunch of violets for Thetis.*] The witch woman is mad lest any hurt come to the boy!

ALCIMEDON.

Health to you, Priest, and discretion to your tongue!

PRIEST.

Health I accept, Alcimedon,—discretion to them that need it!

ORESTES.

[*To the* PRIEST.] Why, what should bring hurt to the lad?

ALCIMEDON.

[*Carelessly, passing on.*] Jealousy stranger. Priests and barren women!

> [*He passes on to the altar, and then to the rock, where he puts his violets.*

PRIEST.

Jealousy!

ORESTES.

[*Involuntarily.*] Hermione would never plot against the boy!

[*He makes an angry movement after* ALCIMEDON.

PRIEST.

What jealousy? What need to be jealous of him? He is no true heir. We have a King, and we have a Queen, both of the blood of Zeus, both our true rulers, but heir there is none.

ALCIMEDON.

[*Seeing and handling the gold link.*] Ye golden gods, have the sons of Pactôlus us come to Phthia?

ORESTES.

[*In sudden anger.*] The curse of the crawling lichen on the man who moves that gold!

ALCIMEDON.

On your own head! [*Throws gold quickly down.*] Who are you, stranger, to curse one that has done you no wrong?

ORESTES.

I check the wrong before it is done. And I tell not my name save to my host after I have eaten and slept.

ALCIMEDON.

If you come to teach your manners to the Myrmidons, by Thetis! you shall learn theirs first. Is the stranger yours, O Priest?

ORESTES.

I have broken no man's bread nor touched his hand. [*Defiantly.*] What see you more?

ALCIMEDON.

Why is he so bold? Has he sanctuary with Thetis?

ORESTES.

[*Lifting his two spears.*] This is my sanctuary. And there is more gold for the man that will break through it.

PRIEST.

Stay! Slay not the stranger so fast, Alcimedon. Reason with him. He will give up the chain, and we will let him go in peace.

ALCIMEDON.

Go in peace, when he has lifted his spear against Alcimedon! How shall I look my grandchildren in the face? By Thetis! I will wash the chain with his blood!

PRIEST.

Beware; he has spears! It is man to man.

> [*Noise of footsteps.* ORESTES *puts his back towards a rock, so that neither he nor* ALCIMEDON *sees* ANDROMACHE, *the* MAID, *and two other damsels, who enter with pitchers on their heads.*

ALCIMEDON.

[*With his eye on* ORESTES.] Ha! who comes there? [*Calling to the newcomers without looking at them.*] A stranger in arms, and with gold! Ho! Myrmidons!

ANDROMACHE.

Shame on you, Alcimedon, robber of strangers!

ALCIMEDON.

Is it you? [*Yielding reluctantly.*] Nay, he is no man's guest; it is lawful to slay him.

ANDROMACHE.

He is mine. [*To* ORESTES.] Stranger, give me your right hand. [*To* ALCIMEDON.] He is my guest.

ORESTES.

[*Still stormy and excited.*] Shall I take a woman's hand for fear of this old loon? My spear-blade is dry and has not drunk.

PRIEST.

Stranger, you are alone; a wise man chooses peace, and not war.

ORESTES.

Alone? As a wolf among sheep is alone. When he slays first the dog—[*pointing spear at* ALCIMEDON]—and bleeds the sheep as he will!

ANDROMACHE.

And who will be the better when he has bled them? Nay, old friend—[*to* ALCIMEDON, *who wants to break in; then to* ORESTES *again*]—though you slay us all, you have but lost the food and shelter we had given you; and the shedder of blood escapes not the Dread Watchers.

ORESTES.

[*Who had been cooling, starts and threatens her.*] What know *you* of the Dread Watchers?

ANDROMACHE.

And there is little glory in the slaying of a woman, and little gain.

ORESTES.

[*Wildly.*] What woman? Who are you that taunt me? Priest, is this your witch?

ALCIMEDON.

[*Angrily.*] She is no witch! You lie, both stranger and priest!

ANDROMACHE.

I am a bondwoman of the King.

ALCIMEDON.

Andromache, once wife of Hector, Prince of Troy.

ORESTES.

And am I to be the guest of a bondwoman?

ANDROMACHE.

There are others of free estate who will take you in. I only sought to save men's lives.

ORESTES.

What worth are men's lives? I will be guest to none but the King.

ANDROMACHE.

One of these will guide you, when you will, to Pyrrhus' castle.

ORESTES.

[*Relaxing suddenly.*] Oh, let me be.

[*He sits down on a rock, and buries his face in his hands.*

ANDROMACHE.

[*To* ALCIMEDON.] The man is very weary and sore at heart, Alcimedon.

PRIEST.

It may be he is mad. It is well we hurt him not.

ALCIMEDON.

Banishment may make a man well-nigh mad. I remember the year of my own manslaying.

ANDROMACHE.

Perchance he has been long alone in the forests. Take him and give him food and drink.

ALCIMEDON.

The priest can take him. I want no more of the man.

ORESTES.

[*Wearily.*] Nay, touch me not. Leave me awhile.

PRIEST.

[*To the others.*] It is well. Make your prayers.

ANDROMACHE.

[*Approaching the altar, and praying with upstretched hands.*] Greeting to thee and joy, Thetis, mother of all Phthia. Give us peace in this land; and grant that my son Molossus return safe, and grow to give joy to thee and all this house!

ALCIMEDON.

[*In the same way.*] Joy to thee, Thetis! Accept my offerings, and grant that my arms keep strong, and that I find the man whose swine have trampled my barley field.

MAID.

It will be a long day before Thetis grants you that, old man.

ALCIMEDON.

[*Grumbling.*] If I only knew of any one that knew!

PRIEST.

[*To* FIRST MAID.] Have you a prayer to make?

MAID.

[*Taking offerings from other* MAIDS *to add to her own.*] Hail, Thetis! and may joy be ever with thee! Accept these offerings from the bondmaidens Aithra, and Pholoe, and Deianassa; and grant all good things to them and theirs. [*A pause.*

ALCIMEDON.

The jade! She is praying in silence! Ho, stop her, Priest! [*The others giggle.*

MAID.

'Tis as good as a witch's prayer, at the worst!

ALCIMEDON.

[*Taking hold of her and threatening her with the shaft of his spear.*] Say it aloud, now! Say what it was!

MAID.

I won't! I won't! Let me be. It was no harm.

ANDROMACHE.

Let her be.

ALCIMEDON.

Swear it was nothing touching me, nor my crops, nor those swine!

MAID.

By Thetis! I think not of you, nor your crops nor your swine!

ORESTES.

[*Recovering from his reverie.*] Well, lead me in. I will be the guest of any that will take me.

PRIEST.

You have given an offering, stranger; you may pray if you will.

ORESTES.

I—to Thetis! No! Yet perhaps—— [*Going up to altar.*] Hail, Thetis! I have given thee an offering of many oxen's price, and many more will I give if thou hinder me not of my desires.

ALCIMEDON.

A vile prayer, a very dangerous prayer! He might as well have prayed silently. I will not take the man; the Priest may take him. [*The* PRIEST *goes towards* ORESTES.

ORESTES.

[*Looking about and scanning the faces.*] I will be this bondwoman's guest.

ANDROMACHE.

So be it, stranger. [*The* PRIEST *moves anxiously towards* ORESTES.] And perchance the Priest will give you shelter till my work is done.

PRIEST.

Ay, come with me. When the King returns, it were meeter that he should take you. [*Aside to* ORESTES.] Beware, stranger! It is the Phrygian woman.

ORESTES.

[*Apart to* PRIEST.] She is over-wise, methinks; but not evil. I fear her not. [*Coming back as though on impulse.*] I give you my hand, wife of Hector!

ANDROMACHE.

It is well, my guest. [*Taking his hand.*

PRIEST.

Till the King returns! [*Exeunt* PRIEST *and* ORESTES R.

ALCIMEDON.

[*As* ANDROMACHE *and the women draw water at the well.*] Lazy hounds, to let Hector's wife draw water! Fill her pails for her, little foxes!

FIRST MAID.

Better *she* fill mine! Perhaps she knows charms for filling them.

ANDROMACHE.

It is well, fellow slave. Let our work be even.

> *Enter, by the path from the Castle,* HERMIONE, *with two attendants carrying libations. She does not notice the slaves.*

ALCIMEDON.

Greeting, O Queen.

HERMIONE.

Greeting, old man. [*Going up to the altar.*] Hail, Thetis, and have joy! Accept this wine and the blood of an ewe with two lambs that I bring to thee; and take off from me, I beseech— — [*She stops, looks round, and sees* ANDROMACHE, *on whom she turns with vehemence.*] You? [*Flings out the blood on the ground.*

ALCIMEDON.

Queen, you have flung out the blood upon the ground!

HERMIONE.

What would my sacrifice profit, with that woman's eyes upon me? [*To* ANDRO-

MACHE.] Get you back to the castle! Is the water not drawn yet?

ANDROMACHE.

I go, O Queen!

ALCIMEDON.

You are over-proud, my Queen, over-proud.

HERMIONE.

May a Queen in Phthia not give commands to her own slaves?

MAID.

[*At the shrine.*] Holy Aphrodite! some one has put gold upon the shrine!

ALCIMEDON.

'Twas a stranger that the Priest has taken in. Have a care: the dog laid a curse on any who should move it.

HERMIONE.

A stranger! He comes from the South, then; from Athens, or Argos, or Mycenæ — —

ALCIMEDON.

No, Queen, he is only an Acarnanian. But belike he has journeyed to the South.

HERMIONE.

That is no Acarnanian gold! [*Taking it up.*] See you the sea-beast wrought on it, with many feet? [*To* MAID.

MAID.

Yes, but the curse, Queen — —

HERMIONE.

[*Not heeding her.*] It brings my home back to me. In Lacedæmon we all wore chains of gold about our necks.

MAID.

Queen, the man laid a curse upon it!

HERMIONE.

[*Putting it back.*] I meant no evil; and that dear gold of the South will never hurt me — — In Agamemnon's palace the men had gold in their armour, and even in the blades of their swords! And the gold was wrought into lions and wild bulls and trees, and strange sea-beasts like this.

ALCIMEDON.

A plain haft and a plain blade cuts the steadiest.

HERMIONE.

[*Angrily.*] Bah! You deem because you are rude you are valiant, Alcimedon! The soldiers of the South were as brave as you.

ALCIMEDON.

[*Turning away towards the maidens.*] Let not Andromache draw the water, jades!

HERMIONE.

Will you not draw for her yourself, old man?

ALCIMEDON.

I draw water! [*Drawing himself up in indignation.*] By Hermes! I care not for the tongue of a barren woman.

[*Voices and the loud talk of huntsmen are heard outside.*

VOICE OF MOLOSSUS.

Ho! Mother, Mother!

MAID.

[*Looking.*] It is Molossus! And the King's huntsmen. They are coming up the path.

ALCIMEDON.

Already!

HERMIONE.

[*To* ANDROMACHE, *who has stopped.*] Why do you wait? Have I not bidden you back to the castle? And when the hall is swept, go to your own house. Come not up to trouble the King till that web is finished.

ANDROMACHE.

[*Turning again and moving away.*] I go, O Queen.

VOICE OF PYRRHUS.

[*Outside.*] Ho, wife of Hector, mother of Molossus! Stay, and look at him.

MOLOSSUS *and* PYRRHUS *enter, with some spearmen;* PYRRHUS *has his arm on the neck of* MOLOSSUS.

MOLOSSUS.

[*Running forward.*] Mother, look! I have slain a man!

PYRRHUS.

He has slain his first man.

> [MOLOSSUS *holds up his hands, the palms of which are smeared with blood.*

MOLOSSUS.

See, mother; they have smeared me with his blood!

HERMIONE.

[*Holding aloof.*] Keep away from the altar, with foul hands!

ANDROMACHE.

[*To* PYRRHUS, *with reproach, while she embraces* MOLOSSUS.] You said you would take him to no battles, only to hunting.

PYRRHUS.

[*Cheerily.*] By Hermes, it was he who made the battle! I meant nothing but hunting.

ALCIMEDON.

Well done, boy! A true prince, a true prince!

PYRRHUS.

We had driven the deer down over the mountains and we came on a herd of the Napæans' cattle grazing, right up on the moors.

ANDROMACHE.

You promised me you would raid no cattle with him.

PYRRHUS.

By Hermes! They *came* to us! And the herd-boy never saw us; he was sitting on a stone in the sun, and thinking of nothing. And even then I would not raid the cattle. When suddenly up jumped the herd-boy and looked at us, with his mouth open. And before he knew who we were, I heard a twang!—and there he was with an arrow in his neck! [*Laughs.*

MOLOSSUS.

Right through his throat, mother! He was looking up. [*Imitating the attitude.*] And I have got a pipe he was plaiting. It wasn't finished, but it blows. [*He shows a pipe made of reeds.*

PYRRHUS.

You can play better things than pipes, my boy. So we ran down and cut off the cattle; and I have given them to Molossus for his own herd.

MOLOSSUS.

And father put the blood on my hands himself.

PYRRHUS.

I will do more for you than that, my firstborn.

HERMIONE.

[*Who has kept back, by the altar.*] Take up your pitcher, and begone, woman!

PYRRHUS.

[*Turning upon* HERMIONE.] Now, by Peleus, daughter of Helen, what would you?

HERMIONE.

That when my slave is gone you may give me greeting.

PYRRHUS.

I give you greeting. But I praise not your greeting to me.

HERMIONE.

If I send my women to draw water at sunrise, shall the water not be back when the shadows are thus? [*Pointing to shadows.*

PYRRHUS.

There be other women meeter to draw water than Hector's wife. I tell you there is no man on this earth I should so joy to have slain as Hector.

HERMIONE.

If he had witchwork to help him, he may have been a deadly fighter.

ANDROMACHE.

[*To* PYRRHUS, *who has laid his hand on her shoulder.*] Nay, master, the hall must be made ready.

PYRRHUS.

Well, take our boy, and be with him at the castle when I come. Stay, think of a boon to ask of me in return for the day's good work. And make it a rich boon; I shall not stint you.

ANDROMACHE.

I know it now; but I fear to anger my lord.

PYRRHUS.

Ask on; yet I would not have you ask for freedom from me.

ANDROMACHE.

My master, what could I do now with freedom? Only suffer Molossus to make atonement to the Napæans for the man he slew. He may give back the oxen, and I will add of my own.

PYRRHUS.

[*Displeased.*] Atonement! Who are the Napæans to seek atonement from me?

ANDROMACHE.

Nay, my lord, it was scarce a righteous slaying.

PYRRHUS.

Not righteous! [*Scornfully.*] Then perchance you would have me cut off the herd-boy's hands and feet, for fear his ghost should come after us? Not righteous! What is it you fear?

ANDROMACHE.

[*Putting her hand on* MOLOSSUS' *shoulder.*] He is but a boy, my lord! And if there is no atonement, they will watch day and night to slay him.

MOLOSSUS.

Mother, I fear them not!

ANDROMACHE.

They will raid us again— —

PYRRHUS.

I can do them twice and four times the hurt they can do me.

ANDROMACHE.

They cannot hurt *us* in our castle, but they can burn the villages in the plain and make dearth and famine.

Molossus.

Oh, Mother, why should I make atonement for my first man?

Pyrrhus.

It was only a boy, too. I cannot ask forgiveness for one boy!

Andromache.

It will cost little. I have three carpets of Sidon work— —

Pyrrhus.

And the oxen! I have given them to the lad; and one is already eaten. Well, well, it is for the lad to say if he will give back his oxen and ask for pardon.

Hermione.

[*With a ring of emotion in her voice.*] Shall my chests be made empty because your slave's child is afraid?

Molossus.

I am not afraid. I will never atone!

Pyrrhus.

[*To* Hermione.] Peace, O Queen! [*To* Andromache.] Go! If Molossus wills, he can make his atonement. On to the castle, men! [*Exeunt spearmen.*

Andromache.

[*Turning as she goes off.*] Be not wroth, my King. Your hall would be very desolate if the boy were slain. [*Exeunt* Andromache *and* Molossus.

Hermione.

There is another atonement should come first, if you must humble yourself.

Pyrrhus.

[*Stopping as he is going off.*] What other?

Hermione.

Atone to Orestes, Agamemnon's son, that you stole away his bride!

Pyrrhus.

[*Firing up and laying his hand on his dagger.*] Daughter of a dog! I stole no man's bride.

Hermione.

Was I not vowed and sworn to Orestes?

PYRRHUS.

Your father vowed you, not I. What is it to me if your father broke his oaths?

HERMIONE.

You helped him and bribed him to break them. The wrath of the Broken Oath is on both of you!

PYRRHUS.

You are mad, woman. Orestes had murdered his mother, and the Spirits without Name haunted him day and night — —

HERMIONE.

My father knew that when he betrothed me. He could be purified.

PYRRHUS.

[*Scornfully.*] Purified? For slaying his mother?

HERMIONE.

And you, you dared not enter the land while Agamemnon's son was there; you waited till — —

PYRRHUS.

'Twas your father cozened Orestes away. How should I fear Agamemnon's son? Am I not the son of Achilles?

HERMIONE.

And was Achilles a better man than Agamemnon?

PYRRHUS.

All the world knows he was.

HERMIONE.

Then why did all the world choose Agamemnon to be their king?

PYRRHUS.

Bah! Very feeble men may be kings.

HERMIONE.

They may, in Phthia; and beggarly men, and savage, and witch-ridden, and makers of atonement, and stealers of wives!

PYRRHUS.

By Peleus! if I stole you, you were willing. 'Tis yourself you mark with a dog's name, Helen's daughter!

HERMIONE.

God be witness, willing I never was! Though I dreamed not then that I should come to a beggared land and the house of a master who hated me!

> [*Flings herself down by the altar, hidden from the back of the stage
> by the trees.*

PYRRHUS.

By Thetis, woman, you are bewitched!

HERMIONE.

[*With a cry.*] Bewitched! Have I not said it?

> *Enter from* R. *back,* PRIEST *and* ORESTES.

PRIEST.

[*To* ORESTES.] Here is the King himself! [*To* PYRRHUS.] Son of Achilles, I bring you this stranger, whom your handmaid, Andromache, commended to my care.

PYRRHUS.

Whence comes he, and what seeks he?

PRIEST.

From Acarnania, banished for the slaying of a man.

PYRRHUS.

He seeks not purification?

ORESTES.

The blood is faded long ago from my hand. I seek but to rest a while at your castle; I will give payment either in battle with your enemies, or by tidings and songs from beyond Parnassus and the Waters of Pelops.

> [HERMIONE *looks up in amazement at the voice, utters a stifled cry,
> and peers round.*

PYRRHUS.

It is well, stranger. Tidings are good in peace; and if war comes, an exile for manslaying may well be worth the bread he eats.

ORESTES.

Others know if I am skilled in war. I know only that my life is little worth to me, and I care not much to save it.

PYRRHUS.

A good word, Sir Guest, and worthy of the roof of Achilles. We give you greeting, my Queen and I. [*Shakes his hand, and looks round for* HERMIONE.] Daughter of Helen, have you not seen our guest?

HERMIONE.

[*In a startled tone.*] Seen him? What do you mean, my lord?

ORESTES.

Nay, though methinks I have heard the Queen's praises till it is almost as though I knew her. For the women of the South speak daily of Helen's daughter, and the bards and kings' sons will never forget her.

HERMIONE.

[*Mastering her agitation with difficulty.*] You know the land of Pelops, stranger? It is a fair land.

ORESTES.

Once it was far the fairest upon earth. But now its pride is brought down, and that which made it beautiful is departed. [*He looks steadily at her.*

PYRRHUS.

Ay, they have had their troubles in the South. Howbeit, with us you may stay in peace as long as your pleasure is. Daughter of Helen, give your hand to our guest, and guide him to the castle.

HERMIONE.

[*Moving her hand forward, then drawing back.*] Let another guide him. I have yet a prayer unspoken, and my offering is poured.

PYRRHUS.

[*Displeased.*] Be not vexed, stranger. Who can tell the prayers of a childless woman, save that they change and are very many? Come with me, and to-morrow we will ask your name and race.

[*Exeunt* PYRRHUS *and* ORESTES, L. *The* PRIEST *looks to the niches in the rock to see the offerings.* HERMIONE *falls on her knees at the altar, and prays silently.*

END OF THE FIRST ACT.

THE SECOND ACT

SCENE: *The Hall of* PYRRHUS' *Castle, a rude stone building, with spears, swords, and armour hanging on the walls. A doorway in the back wall leads to the courtyard. At the extreme right is a fire burning; near it are two high seats for the King and Queen.*

On a bench near the door are ANDROMACHE *and* MOLOSSUS *seated; on the floor near them is a small pile of carpets and tapestries, and a bowl with some metal ornaments and small weapons in it.*

ANDROMACHE.

But when you saw him fall, and saw the pain in his face, did it give you no grief?

MOLOSSUS.

A little, it may be. Not more than when I struck my first deer. A child might cry over the ox they are flaying now in the yard.

ANDROMACHE.

And a grown man, too, if it availed anything.

MOLOSSUS.

Mother, you are but a woman, and I am getting to be a man; I must grow past all that and throw it behind me.

Enter ORESTES *unnoticed: he stands in the doorway, leaning against a pillar.*

ANDROMACHE.

May your eyes never see half the pain mine have seen! I grew past feeling for it, too, long, long ago. I saw men writhe and bite the dust, without caring for them or counting them. They were so many that they were all confused, and the noise of their anguish was like the crying of cranes far off; there was no one voice in it, and no meaning. And then, as it went on growing, and the sons of Priam died about me and the folk starved, and my husband, Hector, was slain with torment, all the voices gathered again together and seemed as one voice, that cried to my heart so that it understood.

MOLOSSUS.

What did it say, mother?

ANDROMACHE.

It spoke in a language that you know not, my son.

MOLOSSUS.

Did it speak Phrygian?

ANDROMACHE.

It spoke the language of old, old men, and those whose gods have deserted them.

[ORESTES *moves forward as though to speak, but checks himself.*

MOLOSSUS.

But you could tell me what it said.

ANDROMACHE.

[*Looking at him, and not answering.*] Why did you ever *wish* to kill that herd-boy?

MOLOSSUS.

We had taken their cattle before. They always fight us.

ANDROMACHE.

Would it not be better that they should live at peace with you?

MOLOSSUS.

Why should I fear their blood-feud? I would sooner be slain than ask favours of them. My father would avenge me well!

ANDROMACHE.

And who will be the happier? Listen. Can you hear that little beating sound—down seaward, away from the sun?

MOLOSSUS.

It is the water lapping against the rocks.

ANDROMACHE.

There is a sound like that in the language I told you of. Old, old men, and those whose gods have deserted them, hear it in their hearts—the sound of all the blood that men have spilt and the tears they have shed, lapping against great rocks, in shadow, away from the sun.

MOLOSSUS.

But, mother, no warrior hears any sound like that.

ANDROMACHE.

Hector learnt to hear it before he died.

ORESTES.

[*Coming forward.*] Before he died! Is that its meaning?

ANDROMACHE.

The stranger! [*Turning.*

ORESTES.

Does it mean death, that sound?

ANDROMACHE.

Nay, methinks a man hears it when he has suffered enough, if he has the right ear to hear it.

ORESTES.

But it is then that death should come, when a man has suffered enough.

ANDROMACHE.

Nay, death should not come for suffering. Death should come when there is no hope left for any one thing in the world.

ORESTES.

[*Broodingly.*] One thing!

MOLOSSUS.

But, Mother, they called Hector "Slayer of Men." I want first to slay many, many men, and many wild beasts, and burn a town, that people may fear me, and call me "Slayer of Men." And after that—after that, I will be merciful, and slay only those I hate.

ANDROMACHE.

Shall you hate men still?

MOLOSSUS.

If they wrong me! [ANDROMACHE *smiles.*] Shall I not hate them that wrong me? Do you not yourself?

ANDROMACHE.

Light of my age, if I hated, how should I live? There are three living souls that I love—you and your father and old Alcimus. And if I hated, whom should I hate more bitterly?

MOLOSSUS.

I know my father was your enemy once. But what did old Alcimus?

ANDROMACHE.

He was one of the three who slew my little child.

MOLOSSUS.

Astyanax? [*She nods.*] I wish Astyanax were alive, mother. I would take him hunting.—He would have no share, would he, in my heritage?

ANDROMACHE.

I know nothing of that.

MOLOSSUS.

And did you never hate them—not at the time?

ANDROMACHE.

[*Looking at him, then passing her hand across her face.*] Oh yes, I hated them!

MOLOSSUS.

But not me! I never did much harm to you.

ANDROMACHE.

Some day perhaps you will hurt me worse than any of them; but I shall not hate you.

MOLOSSUS.

[*After a pause, handling the objects in the bowl.*] Well, I give you my oath this time, Mother; but I will not atone for my next slaying.

Enter ALCIMEDON *and Attendants.*

ALCIMEDON.

The bull is finished, and a fine beast he was. [*Seeing the bowl.*] What is this?

MOLOSSUS.

[*Shamefaced.*] Nothing. Some pieces of mother's old stores.

Andromache.

The price for the blood of the herd-boy.

Molossus.

She made me vow it!

Alcimedon.

The atonement? That is right. I feared that Pyrrhus would be too proud to pay it.

Molossus.

You need not think that *I* wanted him to pay it!

Alcimedon.

H'm! That was how *I* talked once, before I knew what a blood-feud was. And now I would pay a dead man's weight in silver to be clear of one. Of course, with a stranger it is different, or a man who has no kin. [*Examining the stores.*] No need to pay too much, though. It was a little boy, they tell me, and poorly clad.

Molossus.

[*Almost crying.*] He was a big boy!—I hate the Napæans, and I will slay more of them!

Alcimedon.

There are the oxen as well. We have killed two; but sorry beasts, both, sorry beasts. Any two calves will more than make up for them.

Molossus.

But I hate them!

Alcimedon.

Hate them your fill; but make up the feud: we must not have Pyrrhus left childless.

Molossus.

What is it to me if Pyrrhus is childless? He can avenge his children.

Alcimedon.

Peace is better.

Molossus.

[*Contemptuously.*] Peace!

ORESTES.

And what is the road to peace? The hate must eat itself out, till it stays for weariness.

ALCIMEDON.

A long road, stranger, too long and too rough to the feet. We want peace *now*!

ORESTES.

How can you get peace now, when the blood is still wet? He may give all his silver and his kine, but he will hate the men whose blood he has drunk; and though they swear by all the gods of their valley, they will hate him. And hate will out, in time, one way or another.

MOLOSSUS.

If ever they swerve a hair's breadth from their oaths——

ALCIMEDON.

And is there to be no peace at all?

ORESTES.

Peace for this one—[*touching* MOLOSSUS]—when Pyrrhus is childless, or when——

ALCIMEDON.

Your words on your own head!

ORESTES.

——when the last of the Napæans has gone from the earth.

ANDROMACHE.

Nay; no peace then.

ORESTES.

Not for the dead?

ANDROMACHE.

Do not men see the dead roaming the world, and hear them call for blood?

ORESTES.

[*Excitedly.*] How know *you*, woman, that the Dead call for blood? [*Gloomily again.*] When the whole of a race is gone there may perhaps be peace.

ANDROMACHE.

But the whole of a race is never gone. Even from Troy there are men escaped who may make cities and seek for vengeance again. And if you blot out all the Napæans, there are those beyond the Napæans who will hate you for that very thing. Make peace, swiftly, before you die, my son, lest there be no peace for ever and ever.

> *Enter* HERMIONE, *with* PRIEST *of Thetis and Attendants; she is richly dressed, and her eyes bright and anxious. She passes up to the two high seats, and takes one. She talks with her* MAIDS, *and* ALCIMEDON *goes over to her.*

ORESTES.

[*Detaching another pendant from his chain.*] Woman, you can see men's hearts, and you talk not as these talk. Behold, there is no peace, for peace is nothing; there is either Love or Hate. [*Throwing pendant into the bowl.*] If gold can buy love where hate is, put that to the blood-gift!

HERMIONE.

[*To* ORESTES, *across the hall.*] Sir Stranger, this Priest tells me you are skilled as a bard.

ORESTES.

I have little skill in music, but I have journeyed much.

HERMIONE.

You can tell us strange tales of your voyages?

ORESTES.

Not of my own. But I was telling this boy a tale even now.

HERMIONE.

Nay, no boys' tales! Andromache, take your son and help with the ox flesh. [*To* ORESTES.] And sit not so far off, among the slaves' seats. Tell us some *man's* story.

ORESTES.

[*Approaching, but bringing* MOLOSSUS *with him, while* ANDROMACHE *goes out.*] Nay, I will keep the boy. It is a boy's tale, this, and of little meaning. But seeing I have begun— — [*To* MOLOSSUS.] Have you heard of a man that once had a great feud—Orestes, Agamemnon's son?

MOLOSSUS.

Who slew his mother, and was driven by— —

PRIEST.

Nay, name them not, child, name not those Holy Ones.

ALCIMEDON.

We love not his name in this house, stranger. Have you no other tale?

HERMIONE.

[*Controlling her excitement.*] Nay, what hurt is his name? It is only some boy's tale.

ORESTES.

He took on him a great feud, greater than he knew. For his father called from the dead for vengeance on the woman who had murdered him. And the gods called, too, and put voices always about him calling for blood. And then they betrayed him!

MOLOSSUS.

Did his father betray him, too?

ORESTES.

Nay, it may be that the voice was not his father's, after all. But the gods——

PRIEST.

See that your tongue offend not, stranger!

ORESTES.

So be it. Well, in the end he recked not of the gods. He cared not how sore they hated him, and cared not if he lived or died.

MOLOSSUS.

And what did he do?

ORESTES.

This is the last story I heard of him, from a Chalcidian man who had been in Sicily.

HERMIONE.

Had he gone so far away?

ORESTES.

Beyond the end of Sicily to a kingdom of the Iberians. For he vowed that he would be like Paris, and win the most beautiful of all women for his wife; for, you must know, the gods had marred all the world for him, and made it all as ashes in his mouth, except beauty. For beauty is immortal, like themselves; and they cannot hurt it. So he sought and questioned where that woman might be; and men said she was queen of a land among the Iberians.

HERMIONE.

[*Half divining his meaning.*] Had he seen her himself?

ORESTES.

Ay, long ago, they said.

HERMIONE.

And did he too deem her so fair?

ORESTES.

[*Looking full at her.*] More beautiful than the flowers and the sunlight, so that in dreams her eyes haunted him.

MOLOSSUS.

Well, and what did he do?

ORESTES.

He took his ship, with a hundred men well armed, and hid them in a bay of Iberia. And he went up alone to the king's castle and saw the woman. For he was not sure if she was really so beautiful, and wanted to see her again very close. So he stayed in the king's house and made a plot to bear her away.

MOLOSSUS.

But what happened?

ORESTES.

I said it was but a boy's story. The Chalcidian knew not what had happened. Some said he won the queen to his ship, and fled away, wandering; and some said she told the king of his plotting, and they slew him there in the banquet hall. [*A slight pause.*] So perchance even Orestes has found his peace; or, perchance he is still an outcast man, with a new feud following him.

MOLOSSUS.

But I wish I knew.

ORESTES.

Oh, 'tis a foolish story, without an ending.

HERMIONE.

[*Breaking out from her suspense; recklessly.*] And a poor fool, your Orestes, whatever befell!

ORESTES.

How so? What if he won the woman?

HERMIONE.

He only fled on the seas with her, an exiled man, with no comfort. Could he not get him a kingdom?

ORESTES.

Belike he cared not for a little kingdom, being once robbed of his own great kingdom.

HERMIONE.

If a high seat is empty, shall not a great king's son be bold to sit on it? Were his men good soldiers of Mycenæ?

ORESTES.

Some, of Mycenæ, who had sacked Troy; some, pirates he had got in his voyaging; all good fighters!

HERMIONE.

Could he not slay that Iberian in his halls, and sit upon his seat?

ALCIMEDON.

By Thetis! that would have been a gallant deed.

PRIEST.

Unrighteous, very unrighteous; but doubtless the Iberian would have sinned against some god!

ORESTES.

The Iberians may be brave fighters; I know not. And he knew of none to help him.

ALCIMEDON.

A hundred good Phthians might have tried it.

HERMIONE.

The queen might have had her own friends who would fight for her.

ALCIMEDON.

A very foul deed, very foul; but a gallant one! And if she would leave her lord—the hound!—she might well help to slay him!

ORESTES.

He did not seek her for her righteousness; he sought her because her beauty spoke like a god to him!

[*A moment's pause. A shout of several voices heard in the Court.*

ALCIMEDON.

What is that shouting?

[*Moves towards door, with* MOLOSSUS; *the* PRIEST *follows.*

HERMIONE.

I heard the King's voice in it. [*To her* MAIDS.] Go, quick. See what has happened. [*They also go towards the door, leaving* HERMIONE *and* ORESTES *alone. An instant of silence; then she makes a quick movement to him.*] Oh, speak!

ORESTES.

Either I will take you this night or I will be slain here in the hall!

HERMIONE.

Oh, take me, take me! I am half dead with wearying!

ORESTES.

You shall weary no more. Go forth alone at midnight to the altar of Thetis——

HERMIONE.

The altar of Thetis—by night! [*She shows fear.*

ORESTES.

What do you fear? [HERMIONE *shudders, but does not answer.*] You dare not? Then, let it end the other way!

HERMIONE.

Dare you slay *him*?

ORESTES.

That is no great thing!

HERMIONE.

And the witch, and the witch-child? [*With frightened ferocity.*

ORESTES.

Slay *her*?

HERMIONE.

You will not? You will not? Oh, then, I dare not go to you!

> [ORESTES *looks at her with surprise and some repulsion; the women and* ALCIMUS *return, followed by* PYRRHUS *and* MOLOSSUS, *with some armour: after them* ANDROMACHE *and some retainers.*

MAID.

A gift for Molossus! The King has given him a helmet and shield and spear!

MOLOSSUS.

And greaves, too, with bronze rims!

PYRRHUS.

Not yet, my boy! [*As* MOLOSSUS *would fit a greave on.*] Bad luck before a banquet.

ALCIMUS.

Wait till the morning, my lad!

PYRRHUS.

[*With sudden displeasure, seeing the blood-gifts.*] What mean all these carpets, and the bowl yonder?

ANDROMACHE.

They are gifts for the atonement.

PYRRHUS.

Atonement—to those dogs!

ANDROMACHE.

My King, it was the boon you granted me.

PYRRHUS.

[*Turning towards* MOLOSSUS.] The boy never consented!

MOLOSSUS.

I—verily I liked it not—but I gave my word. Mother made me.

PYRRHUS.

You have just slain a man, and a woman can frighten you to promising your own dishonour?

MOLOSSUS.

She did not frighten me; she—I know not how she did it!

HERMIONE.

[*With a laugh.*] Others can guess well enough how she did it!

FIRST MAID.

[*Muttering.*] Sorceress!

SECOND MAID.

[*The same.*] Phrygian witch!

ALCIMUS.

Hold your peace, little prating foxes!

FIRST MAID.

Oh, we all know she has witched old Alcimedon, long ago.

MOLOSSUS.

[*Half crying, as* PYRRHUS *stands gloomily silent.*] I would not make atonement to them, Father, for all the world!

PYRRHUS.

She has your word now, little fool; and mine likewise.—By the gods, woman, you have got your will, and shamed me in the eyes of all men.

ANDROMACHE.

Master, your honour is more to me than mine own. This thing shames you not; even Alcimedon deemed it wise and honourable.

ALCIMUS.

The boy is very young; if he were a man, belike——

HERMIONE.

Is Alcimedon the judge of his lord's honour?

ANDROMACHE.

But how should I ever seek to hurt your honour? Why should I wish it?

PRIEST.

[*As* PYRRHUS *goes silently back to the throne.*] A barbarian woman never forgets a hurt.

FIRST MAID.

'Tis the spite of a conquered Phrygian.

HERMIONE.

Let her be, King! She is thinking ever of her Hector, and Astyanax whom you slew!

ANDROMACHE.

My lord — —

PYRRHUS.

Peace, peace! She knows well enough that Hector is dead—and beyond the seas too. Though I were shamed to the dirt in mine own hall, Hector would not hear of it!

HERMIONE.

Are you sure?

PRIEST.

Hector himself is buried beyond the seas, but his ghost may have followed your ships to Phthia. [*Coming up to the throne.*] Yea, son of Achilles, though you like not my counsel, there be witches in Phrygia that can wake the dead, and tell them of shame come to their enemies, or of — —

ALCIMUS.

There be none such in Phthia, old man! And if the dead *should* wake, your prating would even set them to sleep again. [*Laughter, in which* PYRRHUS *slightly joins.*

PYRRHUS.

'Tis well said, Alcimedon! These women and priests!

PRIEST.

Nay, but I *will* speak!

> [*Talks to* PYRRHUS, *round whom a group gathers, leaving* ANDRO-
> MACHE *alone, and* ORESTES *near* ALCIMEDON.

ORESTES.

[*Apart to* ALCIMEDON.] Old man, you have seen Helen. Was she more beautiful than your Queen?

ALCIMUS.

[*Looking towards* HERMIONE, *then brightening.*] Nay, this is a woman like another; Helen was goddesslike, deathless and ageless for ever!

ORESTES.

[*To himself.*] For Helen I could have done it! Alcimedon, did yonder woman ever do Helen any great wrong, anything meet for vengeance?

ALCIMUS.

Andromache? Why, 'twas Helen did *her* all the wrong!

ORESTES.

Even so; and therefore she must have hated her. Did she never seek, think you, to have Helen slain?

ALCIMUS.

I trow not! Why, she gave her home and shelter when the folk of Troy sought to stone her.

ORESTES.

[*Brooding.*] If she had ever plotted against Helen, I could have done it.

PYRRHUS.

[*Shaking off the* PRIEST.] Enough, enough!—Is your stranger in the hall, Andromache?

ANDROMACHE.

He is here, my lord; a man of good counsel, methinks, and like to be faithful to his guest-oath.

PYRRHUS.

He is happily come to a night of festival.—Stranger, you stand far from the fire.

> [ORESTES *and* HERMIONE *have been trying to read one another's*
> *faces. Here* ORESTES *turns bitterly, looks to the suits of armour*
> *on the wall, and chooses a seat near one.*

ORESTES.

Nay, I have a good seat.

PYRRHUS.

We will call the bard and be merry.

ORESTES.

[*Gloomily.*] I have heard your bard but now.

PRIEST.

The stranger makes minstrelsy himself, as many chieftains may.

ORESTES.

Ay, give me a goblet, and I will sing. I am but a rude singer, but my songs may perchance be new.

PYRRHUS.

Take him the wine. [*They bring wine and a lyre.*

ORESTES.

There are two songs running in my ears this hour past; and I know not fully even yet which of the two is better.

PYRRHUS.

Let it be something joyful, meet for a feast-day.

ORESTES.

I fancied before that one of my songs was very joyful; but now methinks there is no joy at all in either.

PYRRHUS.

[*After looking at him questioningly for a moment.*] Then give us a good straight battle-piece, with no cowards in it, and no slaying by stealth.

ORESTES.

[*Excitedly.*] That it shall be! No cowards, no slaying by stealth, and a clean, hard fight! Ay, and it is the easier too!

PRIEST.

You will call first upon the god, stranger.

ORESTES.

Assuredly; and the god can choose the end of the lay. [*Chanting.*

"Lord of Man's hope, whom no man worshippeth,
Heart of his fears, and burthen of his breath,
Queller of hate and love, hear, O Most Strong,

Most Wrathful and Unrighteous, hear, O Death!"

MEN-AT-ARMS.

Good words! Good words!

PRIEST.

God avert the omen! [*He goes and does purifications at the fire.*

ALCIMEDON.

On his own head! By Thetis! this stranger has run over with evil words ever since he came.

PYRRHUS.

Choose another song, Sir Stranger! Men like not the name of Death.

ORESTES.

Not death! Shall I sing of women, then? They come nearest. [*Chants.*

"O Light and Shadow of all things that be,
O Beauty, wild with wreckage like the sea,
Say who shall win thee, thou without a name?
O Helen, Helen, who shall die for thee?"

ALCIMEDON.

[*Starting up.*] Now, by Thetis, stranger, in shape God has made you kinglike, but within a very fool!

HERMIONE.

[*Piteously.*] My mother Helen never *wished* the men to die!

ORESTES.

My singing mislikes you, old man? Or is it women that like you not?

PYRRHUS.

Stranger, some gayer song would better suit a day of rejoicing. Are the songs of Acarnania all sad?

ORESTES.

Do the men of Phthia wince at the name of death?

ALCIMEDON.

We have our own bard, who can sing to our liking; and his lays will tell whether we fear death.

ORESTES.

Your own bard will sing your own valour, belike? That I can ill do; for I have heard but little of the deeds of Pyrrhus.

ALCIMEDON.

The name of Troy has been heard, perchance, even in Acarnania?

ORESTES.

But the praise of your ancestors I could make into something—something gay-er, you said? Was Æacus the first of your house?

ALCIMEDON.

Æacus, son of Zeus.

ORESTES.

[*Twanging the lyre carelessly and improvising.*

    "Great were our sires, and feeble folk are we!
    A strong king and a wise was Æacus,
    And Zeus his father helped him in his need,
    And Pelops, Lord of Hellas, loved him well!"

ALCIMEDON.

[*Grumbling.*] Æacus was no vassal of Pelops!

ORESTES.

    "The son is weaker, weaker than the sire!
    And Peleus he begat, a goodly king;
    Albeit he stabbed his brother on the sand,
    And wandered from his house, and begged, and lied,
    And vowed a goddess held him to her breast."

[*Murmurs in the hall.* ORESTES *pauses and drinks.*

PYRRHUS.

[*Under his breath.*] Does the man seek for strife?

ORESTES.

    "The son is falser, falser than the sire!"——

HERMIONE.

Perchance his wine likes him not. [*Goes down to* ORESTES, *pours him fresh wine, and whispers.*] Are you mad?

ORESTES.

[*In the same tone, looking in her face.*] Knew you not that, long ago? [*Continuing, while she goes back to the throne.*

"Achilles, Peleus' son, was swift of foot,
And slew by guile great Hector, and was slain.
And, though he hid from war in woman's weeds,
And though he kept his tent while others fought,
Yet gat he from his loins one son true born,
And craved not mercy, gave not gifts for blood!"

PYRRHUS.

What does the dog mean?

ORESTES.

"The son is viler, viler than the sire!"

PYRRHUS.

[*Starting up.*] By all my fathers together, this is the end! Ho, Myrmidons!

[*He snatches up the spear and shield of* MOLOSSUS. *The other men
take arms and growl.* HERMIONE *starts up, clasping her head
with both hands, and staring in terror before her.* ORESTES
stays quietly seated.*

ANDROMACHE.

[*Rushing before* PYRRHUS.] Your oath, O King! Your pledged hand! He is our guest!

PYRRHUS.

[*Checking himself suddenly, then turning upon her.*] Whose guest? You brought him here—you gave the barb to his mocking! [*To the men.*] Back, men! [*To* ANDRO-MACHE.] Who taught him to revile my house?

ANDROMACHE.

Nay, I have told him nothing.

MAID OF HERMIONE.

He has been talking hours and hours with the Lady Andromache.

ANDROMACHE.

I know him not. I think he is mad.

BOTH MAIDS OF HERMIONE.

Bewitched, perchance! [*Murmurs of assent and dissent.*

PYRRHUS.

Peace, hounds! [*To* ORESTES.] Sir Guest, this woman has saved you, else, oath or no oath, had I slain you where you stand!

HERMIONE.

[*Starting from her stupefaction.*] What is that in the bowl?

PYRRHUS.

What bowl?

HERMIONE.

The bowl of your blood-gifts. [*Pointing to it.*

PYRRHUS.

My blood-gifts! [*Goes to the bowl; then turns furiously on* ANDROMACHE.] Woman, who gave you this gold?

ANDROMACHE.

No man gave me gold. The stranger cast a pendant of his chain to add to the blood-gifts, for pity, lest the boy should be slain.

PYRRHUS.

Pity of the boy!—'Tis a plot—a plot to shame me past all enduring!

FIRST MAID.

She witched the gold out of him!

PRIEST.

King, King, hear me! She has witched the Queen's womb long ago, and witched the whole harvest. She has this day witched your own boy to consent to your dishonour; she has witched this mad stranger to give her gold worth twenty oxen; yea, she has witched both him and you, so that he stands up and flouts you in your hall. You are stripped naked, O King, for men and dogs to walk upon, that Hector in his grave may be merry!—Judgment, O son of Achilles, judgment!

ANDROMACHE.

Yea, judgment, my King! I, too, crave judgment. Only let not these be my judges.

PRIEST.

Who is she to say how she shall be judged?

ANDROMACHE.

Judge me yourself, O Pyrrhus, son of Achilles! even now, in your anger; and I fear not. Oh, my King, you who know me, say if I have hated you!

PRIEST.

A witch has no right to speak. Let her be bound outside at the gate till she is judged.

ALCIMEDON.

Not speak? What law is this, Priest?

PRIEST.

Not a witch! She will bind the King's heart, so that he cannot judge her.

PYRRHUS.

[*After a moment's hesitation.*] By Zeus in heaven, it is the truth! I cannot judge her while she stands looking at me. Begone, woman!—Nay, touch her not!—Let her go to her own house.

ANDROMACHE.

I go, my King. Yet if you slay me and to-morrow wake sorrowful, bethink you there is no cure for that sorrow! [*Exit* ANDROMACHE.

MOLOSSUS.

Mother, I will come too!

ALCIMEDON.

[*Stopping* MOLOSSUS *at the door.*] To sanctuary! Not to your own house! Take sanctuary, both, at the altar of Thetis, till his fury is over. [*Exit* MOLOSSUS.

ORESTES.

[*Who during the interruption has mounted on the bench, taken the
suit of arms from the wall, and armed himself, here leaps down,
picks up the lyre, and sings again*—

"The son is viler, viler than the sire!"

ALCIMEDON.

The man is armed!

ORESTES.

[*Continuing amid general confusion.*

"Achilles' son slew women and slew babes,

But quailed before the blood-wrath of a churl;
And stole another's bride; and fled, fled, fled!"

[*Tumult in hall.*

ALCIMEDON.

Down with him!

PYRRHUS.

Slay him not! Break his spear and thrust him out!

ORESTES.

Will nothing sting you? Lo, mine was the bride he stole, and from me he fled! For he dared not face the wrath of Orestes, nor the spear of Agamemnon's son.

PYRRHUS.

Orestes!

PRIEST.

Is it Orestes?

ALCIMEDON.

He must have men behind him! To the watch-tower quick! [*Two retainers run out*, R.

HERMIONE.

He lies, he lies! Do I not know Orestes?

PYRRHUS.

Is it not Orestes? Who is it?

HERMIONE.

This is some poor half-mad, wandering minstrel-man. I know him not. He is not Orestes!

A VOICE FROM THE WATCH-TOWER.

There are no men near the castle.

ALCIMEDON.

Well, strike him down!

HERMIONE.

What profit to break the guest-oath for such as he? He is not Orestes!

PYRRHUS.

Now the Furies that haunt Orestes dog you, woman, if you lie! [ORESTES *gives a cry*.

PRIEST.

If he be mad, it were a great sin to slay him. And the god has been strong in him to-day.

HERMIONE.

[*After gazing at* ORESTES *steadily*.] May the Furies that haunt Orestes be ever with me if I lie. [*Recklessly*.] Is that enough? If you would have another oath, behold, I will go this night to the altar of Thetis——

PYRRHUS.

Hush, Queen, lest the goddess hear!

HERMIONE.

[*Continuing*.] And there by the altar I will swear oaths, and Thetis may work upon me what she will!

PYRRHUS.

Nay, daughter of Helen, no such wild words! I mistrust you not.—Guest, get you gone in peace.

ORESTES.

[*Subdued by mention of the Furies*.] I go, not fearing you, but lest I see Them. I am no guest of yours. [*Throwing down armour*.] Take back your shield and helmet. Aught else I have had from your hands, my gold will more than repay [*With horror*.] Apollo, Averter of Evil! keep them back!—Oh, why did you not slay me while you might? [*Exit* ORESTES.

A RETAINER.

Shall we not stone him from the Court?

PRIEST.

He is possessed! Stricken of God! Touch him not if you fear the gods' anger.

HERMIONE.

[*Terrified, staring in front of her*.] No, no, I see nothing!

END OF THE SECOND ACT.

THE THIRD ACT

SCENE: *As in Act I. Night.* ANDROMACHE *on the steps of the altar of Thetis, with* MOLOSSUS *asleep. Enter from the back, one after another, three armed men, with bows and arrows as well as spears; they pass silently behind rocks or bushes and disappear. Enter* ORESTES, *armed, by path at back: a* MAN *comes from behind a rock to meet him.*

ORESTES.

Is the watch set?

MAN-AT-ARMS.

Everywhere.

ORESTES.

And the path to the ship safe?

MAN-AT-ARMS.

Yes. We have but to wait till they are drawn off from the castle.

ORESTES.

Which way will Pylades lure them?

MAN-AT-ARMS.

He will feign flight northwards, to leave our way clear to the ship.

ORESTES.

Good. One thing more. If I be stricken here, waste no men's lives for me. Make your way back to the ship.

MAN-AT-ARMS.

Prince, we have our orders for this night's work from Pylades. We leave you not.

ORESTES.

Nay, what worth is a dead body, or who can hurt it?

Man-at-Arms.

Hush! What was that?

[*Steals back to his ambush.* Andromache *has made some movement.* Orestes *peers towards Castle,* l., *in darkness; then, turning, sees that there is a woman at the altar.*

Orestes.

Daughter of Helen, why at the altar? Whom do you fear so sore? [*No answer. He comes nearer and sees* Molossus *lying.*] What does the boy here?

Andromache.

It is the stranger! Come you to seek *me*, or what more has chanced?

Orestes.

Is it you? You?—Is the boy asleep?

Andromache.

We have waited here so long, and have heard no word, good or evil.

Orestes.

But why hide you here?

Andromache.

We have taken sanctuary from the wrath of the King and Queen, my guest.

Orestes.

Call you me still your guest?

Andromache.

Nay, you are still my guest till you leave the land; and the King's wrath will perchance be cooled to-morrow.

Orestes.

Why did you not let them slay me in the hall? 'Twas your own folly. I sought no hurt to you. Speak, think you an altar will hold me back, or your blood stain deeper than my mother's blood?

Andromache.

Who are you that speak like this? And what will my death profit you?

Orestes.

Spoke I not loud enough in my enemy's hall? I am Orestes.

ANDROMACHE.

[*Amazed.*] Clytæmnestra's son! [*Coming towards him.*] Oh, now I understand your face! Give me your hand. Whether that old stain be yet purged or no— —

ORESTES.

'Tis hidden and buried, rather, with much new blood over it. [*Keeping back his hand.*

ANDROMACHE.

It is such a one as you I have long prayed for, to be a friend to my child and me.

ORESTES.

Why should I be your friend? I want no friends.

ANDROMACHE.

Listen. You and I have had more grief than others. We have seen beyond the glory of battle, beyond the joy of the conqueror and the shame of the conquered— as Priam and Hector saw before they died.

ORESTES.

I know the battle, and I know the shame. I have seen nought else.

ANDROMACHE.

The King has had but little sorrow; he has conquered always, and taken glory in his manslaying.

ORESTES.

Belike he will soon taste the other side of glory.

ANDROMACHE.

It may be. But none here, save old Alcimus, know aught of suffering. I have long prayed that some man should come here who had suffered from the hurts he had done, and learnt to pity men and women. And if the King's feet are set fast and cannot be turned, at least there is my son.

ORESTES.

Woman, I am come to slay the King and your son!

ANDROMACHE.

[*Calmly.*] Slay them? But why? Why?

ORESTES.

To take their kingdom, as others have taken mine!

ANDROMACHE.

But is all the grief wasted that the gods have sent you? Can you not forget past evils and live in peace?

ORESTES.

In storm I can forget them. Peace is all anguish to me.

ANDROMACHE.

And what will a kingdom profit you?

ORESTES.

I am a king's son; I must have my kingdom.

ANDROMACHE.

Oh, you kings and kings' sons, you dwell like wolves in your castles. I have heard many a ploughman at his ploughing sing with gladness, but seldom, seldom, a king's son.

ORESTES.

Wolves must live in the wolves' way; and they have their own gladness, too.

ANDROMACHE.

You may know them by the howling of their misery in the night! God grant my boy may never be a king!

ORESTES.

Shall I slay him, then, as they bid me? Or would you that I should take him away, where there are no kingdoms? My ship is in the bay, and lacks not for plunder.

ANDROMACHE.

Better that you should slay him now, where he lies.

ORESTES.

Is he asleep? [*He bends tenderly over* MOLOSSUS; *then recovers himself, and speaks in a harsh troubled voice.*] Why is it that you fear me not?

ANDROMACHE.

Why should I fear you?

ORESTES.

Do you trust to these gods? For I reck little of them.

ANDROMACHE.

Nay, my gods are vanished and powerless long ago, and these are but my enemies' gods.

ORESTES.

Then what defence have you against me?

ANDROMACHE.

I need no defence. You and I are friends.

ORESTES.

How, friends! I am charged to slay you also.

ANDROMACHE.

You will not slay me.

ORESTES.

How can you know what I myself know not yet?

ANDROMACHE.

You have no peace to see your own heart; but I can see it.

ORESTES.

How have you learnt it? — Woman, they may well speak of your sorceries!

ANDROMACHE.

I have no sorceries. This is a simple thing. We slaves learn to read men's moods in their eyes and voices, because their moods bring life or death to us.

ORESTES.

Then why do you not fear me the more? [*Roughly.*]
You have never seen my heart!

ANDROMACHE.

He who has seen beyond the glory of bloodshedding may soon see beyond the hardness of man's heart.

ORESTES.

[*Troubled — roughly.*] I know my own heart!

ANDROMACHE.

The gods' hearts may be hard, but man's is tender; only very hungry, and sore afraid, and wild as a hunted beast on the mountain.

ORESTES.

Know you your Queen's heart?

ANDROMACHE.

Not hard, but starving. And she thinks, perchance, that the grief of others will feed it.

ORESTES.

[*Absently—bending and touching the boy's hands.*] He is very cold.

Enter HERMIONE, *hooded and wrapped, hurriedly.*

HERMIONE.

[*To herself.*] Is there no one?—Oh, I dare not!

[ORESTES *steps quickly out from behind the trees.* HERMIONE *starts in terror.*

ORESTES.

Welcome, daughter of Helen!

[HERMIONE *does not answer, but stands, breathing hardy with relief.*

ORESTES.

Throw back your hood.—Ye gods, she is passing beautiful!

HERMIONE.

Take me quick to the ship. Quick, quick!

ORESTES.

It is not yet time. My men must draw Pyrrhus away from the castle.

HERMIONE.

He has gone. Nay, take me quick—Orestes——

ORESTES.

Why do you tremble so? What is it?

HERMIONE.

That oath I swore— —

ORESTES.

You have not heard Them?

HERMIONE.

I know not. There seemed shapes at the edge of the trees.

ORESTES.

Shapes! [*Looks at her close.*] No; *you* have not seen them.

HERMIONE.

[*With horror.*] Is the sight of them written on men's faces?

ORESTES.

Speak not of them!—You have neither seen nor heard.

HERMIONE.

It is only now, and here, that I am afraid. Take me to the ship now; and when once it is over— —

ORESTES.

When Pyrrhus is slain?

HERMIONE.

And the other—[*clinging to him*]—oh, then we shall be safe and at peace.

ORESTES.

The boy? Why do you fear him?

HERMIONE.

[*Absently.*] The boy? He is the king's son.

ORESTES.

But why do you *fear* him?

HERMIONE.

It is not the boy I fear.

ORESTES.

Who, then?

HERMIONE.

It is the woman.

ORESTES.

[*Repelled.*] And what fear you from *her*? I care not to slay a woman and a child.

HERMIONE.

I can never breathe in peace while she is there!

ORESTES.

[*Sternly.*] What has she done?

HERMIONE.

[*Speaking in vague, troubled tones.*] When she is near me, even if I know it not, her breath runs in my blood and makes me tremble. [*She is trembling.*

ORESTES.

Be still! Say what she has done. If she has done you a wrong I will slay her.

HERMIONE.

[*In the same way.*] I might have borne her eyes perchance in my own country, with friends near me; but here, all alone— —

ORESTES.

What has she done?

HERMIONE.

[*In the same way.*] I meant no hurt to her for her sharing the king's bed. But when first I saw her and she looked straight into me, there was something that turned my heart sick and dimmed my eyes.

ORESTES.

How can I slay her for dreams like these? I know nought of your heart, but I can see your beauty. She has not hurt that.

HERMIONE.

Can you not see a dimness over my face, where it once was bright—and a radiance in hers?

ORESTES.

[*Reflecting.*] There is a radiance, although she is so sad.

HERMIONE.

Where got she that radiance? It is not hers. It is the joy and sunlight she has sucked out of me!

ORESTES.

[*Looking at her coldly.*] I can see no cloud in your face.

HERMIONE.

[*Passionately.*] No, no, you cannot see. I am rotting, shrivelling, dying within; and only she can see how I die!

ORESTES.

All flesh must decay. Tell me one deed of hate she has done, and I will slay her.

HERMIONE.

She has made me childless, that her child may be king!

ORESTES.

[*To himself.*] And Helen never faded at all.

HERMIONE.

Childless, barren—barren of womb and of heart!—I had courage and strength to bear good sons, till she sapped it from me to feed *her* son. Nay, there is another thing——

ORESTES.

[*Coldly.*] What?

HERMIONE.

No, no, you do not believe me! I cannot say it.

ORESTES.

You speak such wild things.

HERMIONE.

I know not why I am so wild now, and anger you.—When she is near, it makes me wild and cruel; but now, I know not why this should come over me.

ORESTES.

Great Zeus! if it should be true!—Andromache, Andromache, speak and answer her.

HERMIONE.

Is she here? [Andromache *comes out from the trees by the altar*.] Averter of Evil, what is that?

ANDROMACHE.

I am but your handmaid, I have done you no hurt.

HERMIONE.

Nay, now you can see it—the thing I dared not say!

ORESTES.

What is it?

HERMIONE.

She is no live woman! See! she is dead and sucks the blood of the living. Why is she not afraid, like a live woman?

ORESTES.

[*Troubled.*] She is deathly white. Why she has no fear I know not.

ANDROMACHE.

What can I answer? The King might slay me, but not this man.

ORESTES.

It was the same but now, when I held death over her.

HERMIONE.

She has passed through death! She has no fear, no anger, as the living have. Why does she never ask for anything? [*Almost beside herself with terror.*] Faugh! the smell of death clings about all her garments! Kill her, kill her! [ORESTES *looks at* HERMIONE *with a shudder.* HERMIONE, *breaking down, continues.*] Oh, friend, friend, I was not like this in Sparta.

ANDROMACHE.

Queen, I know my heart is with the dead of Troy. Why should that anger you?

ORESTES.

[*Looking at* HERMIONE.] In very truth there is a shadow come over you. You seem to be shrunken, and scarce so wondrous beautiful.

HERMIONE.

[*In a weary frightened voice.*] Kill her, kill her!

ORESTES.

I know not— —

HERMIONE.

You have eyes. Can you not see there is a fiend working in me?

ANDROMACHE.

There is no fiend. Queen, Queen, why are you so full of hate?

HERMIONE.

'Tis your spells have done it! Before I came here I never hated any one.

ORESTES.

[*To* ANDROMACHE.] Know you not any cause why she should hate you?

ANDROMACHE.

Nay, stranger, why *do* men hate?

HERMIONE.

She has made me feel that I am vile. Slay her, or I go back to the King.

ORESTES.

Pyrrhus most like is dead. If I do slay her will you come away with me?

HERMIONE.

Away? To the ship? Yes; till we come back and take the kingdom!

ORESTES.

I will not take your kingdom!

HERMIONE.

Is it the boy you fear to slay?

ORESTES.

My kingdom must be an ever-changing kingdom. I dreamed for an hour that I might stay and rest like other men.

HERMIONE.

And why not?

ORESTES.

There be Those watching that will not let me rest.

HERMIONE.

Those watching? But you have not seen them? *I* have not seen anything! [*To herself.*

ORESTES.

Not now. Few men have ever seen them; but I hear their wings on the wind. And perchance if I stayed long in one place— —

HERMIONE.

I hear nothing. [*Listening.*] No, it cannot be wings on the wind! Oh!

ANDROMACHE.

Nay, there is no sound at all. Be not so terrified.

HERMIONE.

I cannot stay here alone! Oh, I care not for the kingdom.

ORESTES.

We are exiles for ever, both!

HERMIONE.

Nay, if you love me I can bear anything; if any one will love me.

ORESTES.

I know not if I love or hate you. It was for your passing beauty I came, because your eyes beaconed me through the dark of the sea.

HERMIONE.

Oh, take me; that is all the love I want!

ORESTES.

Like those two stars that men call Helen's brethren, immortal, never fading— —

HERMIONE.

Oh, I am fading fast, but, perchance, if the spell were off me— —

ORESTES.

Nay, you shall never fade. There is a blue sunlit island, waterless, desolate— Hear me, daughter of Helen, ageless and deathless!

HERMIONE.

I hear.

ORESTES.

Some sunset when you are beautiful like a dream I will set you on that bright island, and fill my eyes full. And then I will go my ways alone, and the fairest of earthly things shall be mine for ever.

HERMIONE.

What do you mean?

ORESTES.

No man shall ever see you fade from your loveliness. The gods may take you even as they took Helen.

ANDROMACHE.

Oh, he is mad! Queen, Queen, go back while there is time.

HERMIONE.

[*Shrinking back.*] I should die! I am afraid!

ORESTES.

Die? Of that I know not. Only never, never fade; perfect for ever without age or waning! Daughter of Helen, will you come with me? [*A sound of arms outside. They start.*

HERMIONE.

Oh, quick! I am yours. Do with me what you will.

ORESTES.

Come. [*Sound again.*] What is that?

VOICE OF PYRRHUS.

Andromache! Ho! snake of Phrygia, starve at the altar if you will! Your plotters are all fled!

[ORESTES *stands in posture of defence.* HERMIONE *shrinks back.*

ANDROMACHE.

[*To* MOLOSSUS.] Cling fast! [*Rushing from the altar towards* PYRRHUS.] Back, my king! Keep back!

HERMIONE.

[*To* ORESTES, *with a cry.*] Now, now! [*Hides her face.*

MOLOSSUS.

[*Waking up slowly.*] Is that father coming?

PYRRHUS.

[*Entering and grasping* ANDROMACHE.] Think you to die so easily? You shall speak first and tell all!

ANDROMACHE.

There is an ambush! Keep back!

[PYRRHUS *stands with his sword drawn over her.*

PYRRHUS.

[*Looking up.*] More treachery?

ORESTES.

Why is the son of Achilles away from the battle?

PYRRHUS.

You? Pirate! Because your men fled so fast and so far. My servants have chased them twenty furlongs from here. Yield!

ORESTES.

[*Loud.*] No man shoot nor stir! [*As before.*] Your Myrmidons may be twenty furlongs from here; my men are in these thickets to right and left. What sought you here? Was it to slay Andromache?

PYRRHUS.

I sought that when I came. Now I need more.

[*He poises his spear.* ANDROMACHE *slips back to* MOLOSSUS *at the altar.*

ORESTES.

[*Not raising his spear.*] Nay, it was I that should have slain Andromache. Go your ways! I only take back my own bride.

[*Pointing to* HERMIONE, *whom* PYRRHUS *now sees for the first time.*

PYRRHUS.

It *is* Orestes!—But the queen vowed—— And that oath! Oh, perjured! perjured!

HERMIONE.

[*To the rocks and thickets.*] O ye in the ambush, strike him down! Strike him down! Oh, what is that rushing on the wind?

> [*Puts her hands over her ears as though in terror.*

ORESTES.

The oath is fulfilled upon her!

ANDROMACHE.

[*Close to* PYRRHUS.] My lord, my lord, wait and let him speak. It is he that asks you, so there is no dishonour. [*He glares at her.*] Nay, you may slay me after if I have done wrong. And his men are crowding behind these bushes and rocks.

PYRRHUS.

[*In a war chant.*] The wolves set an ambush, set an ambush for the lion; and the lion feasted for many days! Ho, Myrmidons!

ORESTES.

They hear you not. Go back!

> [*He grasps his spear for defence;* PYRRHUS *draws his sword and*
> *starts forward.*

VOICE.

[*From behind the rocks.*] Now, men of Mycenæ! [*A shower of arrows strikes* PYRRHUS.

ANDROMACHE.

It is a murder, a coward's murder!

> [PYRRHUS *staggers to the altar and falls.* ANDROMACHE *bends over,*
> *tending him.* MOLOSSUS, *with a cry, snatches* PYRRHUS' *sword*
> *and flies at* ORESTES, *who disarms him at a blow.*

ORESTES.

Hold the boy! Hurt him not!

HERMIONE.

[*In a stupefied tone.*] His blood is running down the steps of the altar!

PYRRHUS.

Where is Molossus? Boy, if you leave these dogs unpunished——

ANDROMACHE.

Nay, curse him not! Oh, my lord, if you have ever loved him, curse him not! Let him be free; he will do all that is well.

Pyrrhus.

[*Faintly.*] Andromache? Ay, then, so be it. It is the same in the end. I am glad I did not slay you, Andromache. [*Dies.*

Hermione.

[*As before.*] His blood is trickling into the mark of the footprint of Thetis! [*Wildly.*] Ah, drag him away, or it will be a curse upon us! He must not die at the altar!

Orestes.

I never slew him. I will not touch a man dying at an altar. Andromache, touch him not; he will haunt you.

Hermione.

She is not afraid of the haunting of the dead. See, she is whispering in his ear. She is doing witchwork to bring him back. [*Crossing to* Andromache, *who is still bending over* Pyrrhus' *body, and kneeling to her.*] Nay, in the goddess's name, Andromache, do not wake him! I have wronged you much, but I will make amends; I will set you free. *He* would never have done that. Only, do not whisper to him! Do not call him back to haunt me!

Andromache.

Hold your peace, traitor and coward! If I *could* bring him back, think you I would stay my voice for you?

Hermione.

O God! And the noise on the wind is nearer and nearer!

Orestes.

[*To* Hermione.] You did not slay him. Even if he does wake, he will only haunt them that slew him.

Hermione.

He saw them not; he knows them not. He has only seen you and me. [*Rapidly.*] Oh, in God's name, it is too much! The sound of Their wings is all about me, and if I dared look, I know I should see Their faces. It is more than one woman can bear. If he wakes I shall go mad!

Orestes.

It is done now. We will fly in the ship quickly; he will never follow us over the seas.

Hermione.

[*As before.*] *She* will show him the way! Oh, she will have no pity! I have sought so long to slay her. She would not spare me now for all the treasures of Egypt. I knew well I should have no peace till I saw her dead.—Oh, woman, woman! bend not over him; whisper to him no more!

ANDROMACHE.

I *will* whisper no more; I will cry aloud—in dead ears, as I have cried all my life! [*To* PYRRHUS.] O thou who hearest me not, who hast never heard me, I call again to thee, let there at last be peace! If thou hast found thy sleep, oh, cling to it! Never wake nor stir to follow these who murdered thee!

HERMIONE.

What does she mean? It is all magic. She means that he *is* to follow us!

ANDROMACHE.

The living have never heard me, and the dead cannot hear; but broken and dying men know the words that I speak. Remember the one moment before utter death, when thine eyes were opened to see and thine ears to hear. Remember that, and forget the long waste of days before!

HERMIONE.

She bids him remember!—He will awake. I can feel that he will wake and follow us!

ANDROMACHE.

By the bitter hate wherewith once I hated thee; by the blood in the streets of Troy and the death-cry of Hector's child; by the love wherewith I have loved thee in spite of all—[*the body moves*]—and love thee still— —

HERMIONE.

[*With a shriek.*] O God! He is waking! [*Grovelling in terror and hiding her eyes.*] Oh, smite off his feet that he shall not pursue, and his hands that he may never lay hold of me!

ANDROMACHE.

Before thy soul is fled far away, hearken to me and put away thine hatred.

HERMIONE.

[*As before.*] Smite off his hands and his feet!

ORESTES.

She is not crying him to waken. She is bidding him rest in peace and not harm us.

Hermione.

It cannot be that; it cannot. I have hated her too sore. It is all witchwork or else madness.

[*She looks up and sees the sword; suddenly clutches it and moves
towards* Andromache.

Andromache.

And afterward go and seek Hector, and he will tell thee more, for he was wiser and greater than other men. And some day this woman, too, will be broken and dying; and then she will see what thou and I have seen, and will know what mercy is. [Hermione *stabs her.*] Ah!

[Andromache *falls over the body of* Pyrrhus. Orestes *starts forward and grasps* Hermione.

Orestes.

[*To the men holding* Molossus.] Hold this wild beast! Let the boy free.

[Orestes *and* Molossus *bend together over the body of* Andromache. *The men-at-arms seize* Hermione.

Molossus.

Mother, speak!—Is she dead?

Orestes.

No, but there is death in her face.

Molossus.

Mother, mother, speak!

Orestes.

[*Standing up.*] We know what she would say — — Young King of Phthia, I never sought to slay your father; and for this woman, I would give all my wealth to have her alive again.—But I will make atonement: take all my gold—[*takes off his chain, and throws it at* Molossus' *feet.* Molossus *stands silent*]—and this dagger likewise. There is a bright stone in the hilt that keeps off the venom of snakes. [Molossus *is still silent.*] And my cloak was woven by women of Sidon. [*Throws down the cloak.*

Molossus.

[*In a struggling sullen voice.*] It was not you that slew her.

Orestes.

Is it the woman? There is your sword. [*Picks it up and gives it him. To the men holding* Hermione.] Hold back her arms, men, that the King may slay her as he will!

[*The men bring forward* HERMIONE, *dazed and stupefied; they hold
her so that either breast or throat may receive the sword.*

MOLOSSUS.

Oh, take her away, or I will verily slay her! Let her never set foot upon this
land again.

ORESTES.

Begone with her to the ship! [*The men move off with her.*

HERMIONE.

[*Suddenly struggling.*] I will not go! Let me free! I will stay and he shall slay me!
[*The men drag her off.*

ORESTES.

And for mine own atonement. [*He looks round.*] Men, get you gone!—If you
would have more, here is my sword; and here is my shield, and my helmet. [*He
lays the arms one by one at* MOLOSSUS' *feet.*]—My men are all gone. The rest is for you
to take.

MOLOSSUS.

[*Looking at* ANDROMACHE.] I will take no more. I will have peace. [*Kneels down,
bending over the body.*

ORESTES.

Peace let it be!—Her face seems strangely joyful.

MOLOSSUS.

I never saw her looking so full of happiness.

ANDROMACHE.

[*Half raising herself, with a radiant smile.*] Hector! Hector!

THE END.

Lector House believes that a society develops through a two-fold approach of continuous learning and adaptation, which is derived from the study of classic literary works spread across the historic timeline of literature records. Therefore, we aim at reviving, repairing and redeveloping all those inaccessible or damaged but historically as well as culturally important literature across subjects so that the future generations may have an opportunity to study and learn from past works to embark upon a journey of creating a better future.

This book is a result of an effort made by Lector House towards making a contribution to the preservation and repair of original ancient works which might hold historical significance to the approach of continuous learning across subjects.

HAPPY READING & LEARNING!

LECTOR HOUSE LLP
E-MAIL: lectorpublishing@gmail.com